Dr. Klinkenfeldt's Guide

to picking up women

by Dr. Klinkenfeldt

Cover art by: Ágúst Bjarklind

Published by: Oz Om Books

Grab hold and lift.

Grab hold and lift.

Grab hold and lift.

Grab hold and lift.

Grab hold and lift.

Grab hold and lift.

Grab hold and lift.

Grab hold and lift.

Grab hold and lift.

Grab hold and lift.

Grab hold and lift.

Grab hold and lift.

Grab hold and lift.

Grab hold and lift.

Grab hold and lift.

Grab hold and lift.

Grab hold and lift.

Grab hold and lift.

Grab hold and lift.

Grab hold and lift.

Grab hold and lift.

Grab hold and lift.

Grab hold and lift.

Grab hold and lift.

Grab hold and lift.

Grab hold and lift.

Grab hold and lift.

Grab hold and lift.

Grab hold and lift.

Grab hold and lift.

Grab hold and lift.

Grab hold and lift.

Grab hold and lift.

Grab hold and lift.

Grab hold and lift.

Grab hold and lift.

Grab hold and lift.

Grab hold and lift.

Grab hold and lift.

Grab hold and lift.

Grab hold and lift.

Grab hold and lift.

Grab hold and lift.

Grab hold and lift.

Grab hold and lift.

Grab hold and lift.

Grab hold and lift.

Grab hold and lift.

Grab hold and lift.

Grab hold and lift.